TRIBES ON THE FRONTIER OF BURMA

TRIBES ON THE FRONTIER OF BURMA

By

FRYER FREDERIC SIR

GYAN

ISBN : 978-81-212-1678-4(HB)

First Published, 1907

Published, 2018

Published by

Gyan Publishing House
5, Ansari Road
Daryaganj, New Delhi-110002
Phone: 011-47034999, 9811692060
www.gyanbooks.com
E-mail: books@gyanbooks.com

Printed at: G. Print Process, Delhi.

TRIBES ON THE FRONTIER OF BURMA

THE CHAIRMAN, LIEUT.-GENERAL SIR EDWIN COLLEN, after making announcements as to the future programme of the Society, said: Very few words indeed will be necessary by way of introduction of the lecturer, for Sir Frederic Fryer is known to us all as a distinguished administrator, whose early years of service were passed in the Punjab, and who has been connected with the great province of Burma for more than twenty-one years. His first service there dates, I believe, from 1886, and although he returned for a short time to the Punjab, where he filled high offices with great distinction, the services of his later years were chiefly in Burma, where he presided over the administration for an unusually long period.

THE popular conception of Burma is, no doubt, that of a flat, level country cultivated with rice, with here and there groves, mostly of teak or palm trees, villages with houses built of bamboo, pagodas and monasteries and wonderful rivers, from which the fertility of the country is derived. This country is supposed to be inhabited by a gay and interesting race called the Burmans, who form the mass of the population. This conception is, no doubt, in a measure correct as regards Lower Burma, except that even in Lower Burma many of the inhabitants are not Burmans, and even in Lower Burma there are two districts, the Salween Hill tracts and the Arakan Hill tracts, which are inhabited, the former by Karens and

Shans and the latter by Chins. On the boundaries of Lower Burma, both east and west, there are chains of mountains, inhabited by hill tribes—Karens, Chins, and others. When you come to Upper Burma, the mountains which form the boundaries of Upper Burma proper on the north, east, and west become plainly visible, and the tribes who inhabit those mountains, though they generally owed allegiance to the King of Burma, are not Burmans at all.

The province of Burma includes, besides Burma proper, the northern and southern Shan States, the small States of Möng Mit, with its dependency Möng Lang, the States of Hkamti Löng, Hsaung Hsup, Sinkaling Hkamti, and the Chin and Kachin Hill tracts, all of which are under the administration of the Government of Burma. Some of these States are small, but the area of the Shan States is 59,915 square miles, and the area of the Chin Hills is 10,250 square miles. The area of the Kachin Hill tracts is computed at 20,000 square miles.

I propose to tell you something of the tribes that inhabit these mountainous regions on the frontier of Burma. The subject is a long one, and I have found some difficulty in compressing my remarks into a paper of moderate dimensions.

In Burma proper there are several non-Burman tribes. The principal of these is the Talaing tribe. They are supposed to have come from South-Western China, and are the earliest representatives of the first of the three known Indo-Chinese immigration waves—the Mon-Annam. Until recently it was supposed that the Talaings were the only representatives of the Mon-Annam people within the limits of Burma. Recent researches have, however, shown that the Palaungs, the Was, and the Riangs or Yins, wild communities inhabiting the north and east of the province, are almost certainly Mon-Annam tribes, who have been forced into the hills by the progress of more recent tides of immigration. The Talaings, who have a language of their own, though it is dying out, were at one time masters of the south of the province, but have had to give way to the more strenuous onrush of younger races, and, being without the refuge of the hills, have been largely absorbed by their Burmese conquerors.

The second of the principal Indo-Chinese waves was the Tibeto-Burman. To it belong the Tibetans, the Burmans (with their comparatively recent offshoot, the Arakanese), the Kachins in the north and north-east, and the Chins on the western hills, and probably also a host of hill tribes, such as the Szis, the Lashis, the Marus, the Lisaws, the Akhas, and the Lahus, who are found scattered over the uplands on the extreme north-east of Upper Burma, and in the north and east of the Shan States. In the case of the Burmans and the Chins, the migratory instinct which brought them from the North has long since died out, but the Kachins are still a useful object-lesson to the student who wishes to realize with what resistless force the prehistoric migration streams must have swept over the face of the land. The southern movement of the Kachin tribes must be a phenomenon of comparatively recent development. Where the wanderings of the race are to terminate remains yet to be seen. The most modern of the three Indo-Chinese immigration waves is that of the Tai, which swept down the valley of the Salween and the Mekong to the east of Burma, to find its ultimate goal on the southern seaboard of Indo-China. To it belong the Siamese, the Laos, several of the hill tribes of French Indo-China, and in Burma the Shans, who, starting from the valley of the Shweli, have spread out during the past fourteen hundred years over the Shan States and across the northern area of Upper Burma westwards to beyond the border of Assam. In Burma proper the Shans have during the last century become to a great extent Burmanized, but in the Shan States they have succeeded in maintaining their identity unimpaired.

Of the origin of the Karens, who now occupy the whole of the eastern frontier of Lower Burma, and are found in large quantities in the region of the deltas, nothing definite is known. Their prehistoric home seems to have been, like that of the other Indo-Chinese races, in or in the neighbourhood of South-Western China. It is beyond doubt that their presence in the country dated back from a very early period, though whether their arrival was before or after the arrival of the Mon-Annams is by no means certain. These are the sole known relic of one of the less defined Indo-Chinese immigration waves, and ethnically occupy a position of singular isolation. It seems probable that they must at some comparatively remote period have undergone an intimate fusion with some of the Mon-Annam tribes. On no other hypothesis is it possible to account for the genesis of the Taungthus, who, though speaking a language which has many affinities with, and has been looked upon as a dialect of, Karen, claim a connection with the ruling class of Thaton, who from time immemorial have been Talaings.

This account of the waves of immigration into Burma I have extracted from the Burma Administration Report of 1901-1902, where it is abstracted from the report of the census taken in 1901. It seems to me to give a very excellent account of the successive waves of immigration which have swept over Burma, and left the races that inhabit it in the position in which we now find them.

KARENS.—The first of the hill tribes with which we came into contact was the Karens. This tribe, as I have said, occupy the whole eastern frontier of Lower Burma, and are found also on the western frontier and in the deltas. According to the last census, the Karens number 727,325 persons, exclusive of the Red Karens, Bres, Padoungs, and Zayeins, who are estimated to number 46,937 persons.

The Karen race is divided into three branches—Sgaw, Pwo, and Bghai or Bwe. The language of each of these three branches is different.

The Karens are spirit-worshippers, though they have traditions of a lost religion. They have readily been converted to Christianity, and when they have adopted the Christian religion they show great self-devotion in subscribing for schools and colleges and for the maintenance of their pastors and teachers. The American Baptist Mission have made, I think, the largest number of converts, but there are many Karens who belong to the Church of England and to the Roman Catholic religion. They are bitterly hostile to the Burmans, who in the days of their ascendancy treated them with harshness and contempt. In the troublous times which followed the annexation of Upper Burma the Karens took the side of the British Government and did very good service.

A battalion of Karens was raised for the military police. They were stationed at Toungoo, but it was found that their pay nearly all went in entertaining friends and relations, who visited them from the hills, so, with their own consent, the battalion was transferred to the Chindwin, where they became restless, and ultimately the battalion was dispersed as a unit, though there are still companies of Karens serving in different battalions of military police.

The non-Christian Karens believe in good and bad spirits, auspices, and omens. To propitiate and influence the spirits they sacrifice pigs, dogs, and fowls to them. From the bones of the sacrificial fowls they derive omens. Like all hill tribes, they lead unsettled lives. They annually clear patches of jungle, which they cultivate after burning the trees and underwood, and when the land becomes exhausted they move to fresh patches of jungle. This method of cultivation is, of course, very wasteful and destructive to the forests.

The Pwo and Sgaw Karens are gradually becoming more settled under the guidance of their pastors, but the Bghai or Bwe Karens, who are commonly known as the Red Karens, are very wild and lawless. Every male belonging to this tribe has the rising sun tattooed in bright vermilion on his back, stretching from side to side across the shoulders. Hence the name of Red Karen.

The Red Karens are diminishing in number owing to the ravages of small-pox. They are ruled by hereditary chiefs. They have given no trouble to the Government since 1888-1889, when an expedition was sent against them, and their then chief, Sawlapaw, was replaced by his next heir, Sawlawi, who has kept very fairly to his engagement with the Government.

The Karenni women wear strings of beads round their neck, waist, and calves, and these strings of beads are so large and stiff that the women can only walk with their legs wide apart and cannot bend their knees to sit down.

The Padaung women wear bands of brass in place of strings of beads, and add to these bands year by year, till their necks become unnaturally elongated. By the time the women are fully grown they carry from 50 to 60, and sometimes over 80, pounds of brass. They wear similar coils of brass on their legs and arms. Round the neck the usual limit of coils is twenty-one. Thus weighted they do all the household work.

It is doubtful whether the Padaungs are really Karens. They are probably hybrids.

SHANS.—North of the Karen country come the Shan States. The Shans, or Tai, are divided into numerous tribes, and they speak different dialects. They have six separate written languages. In none of them are there any Chinese roots.

Their original location was in South-Western China, and they at one time were independent and had a king of their own. Their kingdom, which was called Möng Maolong, was a powerful one. They were conquered by the Burmans as far back as the year 1604. They are now split up into distinct groups, which may be styled the Northern, Southern, and Middle. There are five Northern Shan States, administered by the Superintendent of the Northern Shan States, who is stationed at Lashio.

There are twenty-five Southern Shan States, administered by the Superintendent of the Southern Shan States, whose headquarters are at Taungyi. There are besides fifteen States in what is known as the Myelat, administered by an Assistant-Superintendent, who lives at Thamakan, and who is under the orders of the Superintendent of the Southern Shan States.

The size of the Shan States varies very considerably. The area of Kengtung is 12,000 square miles, whilst the area of Kyong is only four square miles. There are ten States which have an area of less than fifty square miles.

Kengtung is the largest State, but North and South Hsenwi and Hsipaw have also large areas. The rulers of these States are styled Sawbwas, Myozas, and Ngwekunhmus. The title of Sawbwa denotes the highest rank, that of Myoza the second, and that of Ngwekunhmu the lowest rank. The Northern States chiefs are all Sawbwas. In the Southern States there are eleven Sawbwas and fourteen Myozas. In the Myelat there is one Sawbwa and fourteen Ngwekunhmus.

Besides these States there is a Shan State, Möng Mit, under the Commissioner of the Northern Division, and two small States, Hsawng Hsup and Singkalin Hkampti, under the Commissioner of the Central Division. The Shans are all Buddhists, though their Hpongyis, or monks, are singularly lax according to orthodox Burman ideas.

After the death of King Mindon the Shans broke into open rebellion against the rule of King Thibaw. The Kengtung Sawbwa expelled the Burmese garrison from his State, and the Möng Nai Sawbwa overpowered the garrison of Möng Nai. The Shans then plunged into internecine war, and the whole country was a prey to rapine and disorder. After the annexation of Upper Burma, the British Government turned their attention to the Shan States, and by June, 1887, the Southern Shan States had been reduced to order. The Northern Shan States took a little longer to bring into order, but the Hsipaw Sawbwa, the most powerful of the chiefs, was the first of all chiefs to submit. He came down to Mandalay early in 1887, and as an acknowledgment of the example set by him, all tribute from his State was remitted for ten years.

The civil, criminal, and revenue administration of the Shan States is vested in the chiefs of the States, subject to the restrictions specified in the orders of appointment which each chief receives on his recognition or succession. The law to be administered in each State is the customary law of the State, so far as it is in accordance with justice, equity and good conscience, and is not opposed to the law in force in the rest of British India. Power to appoint officers to take part in the administration of any State, and to regulate the powers and proceedings of the chiefs, is vested in the Government.

The Shans are great traders, and bring the produce of their hills down to the plains on pack bullocks. Of late their cattle have suffered from a severe epidemic, and they have been partly deprived of one of their main sources of revenue. A railway to the Southern Shan States, which is much needed to open out the country, has, I hear, been sanctioned. Wheat and potatoes have been introduced successfully into the Shan States, and if a railway is made, supplies sufficient for the whole of Burma can be grown in these States.

The Shans are not the only people who inhabit the Shan States. There are numerous other tribes interspersed in the States, and I will proceed to give a necessarily brief account of some of them.

I must first observe that the inhabitants of the Myelat are not Shans. They are the descendants of Burmese colonists, voluntary or forced. The inhabitants of the Yawng Hwe Lake, who are an amphibious race of men who live on the shores of the lake and on the floating islands formed of reeds in the bosom of the lake, are descendants of a colony of prisoners brought from Tavoy by a King of Pagan many centuries ago. They row their boats in a standing position, holding the paddle with the right leg, which is encircled round the handle.

The Loi Long State is inhabited by Palaungs. Their

villages are always situated high up in the hills and are very secluded. They are supposed to be connected with the Was. The men dress as Shans, but the women wear dark blue cutaway jackets, skirts, and leggings, large hoods with a border of blue, scarlet, and black velvet.

WAS.—The Was, who are of the same stock as the Palaungs, inhabit the country on the north-east of the Shan States. Their location runs for 100 miles along the Salween River, and extends for fifty miles inland from that river up to the watershed between the Salween and Mekhong Rivers. Beyond this watershed, too, they occur in scattered villages. The Was are nominally our subjects, as their country fell to us as a result of the boundary demarcation between Burma and China, which was carried out in 1897-1900. The actual demarcation of the border in the Wa country was not carried out on the ground because of the hostility of the Was.

The Chinese had endeavoured for some years to establish their authority over the Was, who several times appealed to the British authorities to assume control over their country and protect them from Chinese aggression. These appeals were not entertained at the time, owing to the magnitude of the task and the expense which would have been entailed upon the Government should it have placed a permanent garrison in the Wa country. I do not know what the present temper of the Was may be. If, however, it be decided to prolong the Mandalay-Kunlong Railway to its proposed terminus to the Kunlong Ferry, it would be necessary to reduce the Wa country to order; otherwise there would be danger that the Was would attack the railway.

British columns have several times traversed the Wa country. The first visit paid to it by a column was in 1897. The Was were always believed by the Burmans to be cannibals, and, though this belief is now held to be unfounded, there is no doubt that they are keen hunters of human heads.

Their villages are all perched on the slopes of hills or in ravines. Round each village is an earthen rampart from 6 to 8 feet high, overgrown with cactus and other thorny bushes. Behind this rampart is a ditch. The only entrances to the villages are through long tunnels, and there are not more than one or two to each village, and they are secured by doors at either end. Leading to each village, after emerging from the tunnels, are avenues of stakes, to each of which a human skull is affixed. There are often as many as 100 to 200 skulls.

The Was believe that their well-being is entirely dependent upon the possession of skulls, without which they would not be able to grow any crops and would be liable to every sort of misfortune. The head-hunting season is in March and April. Head-hunting must be pursued out of their own country, and the greater the prowess of the tribe from which a skull is procured the greater is its value. It may be easily understood that the Was are not pleasant neighbours. The Was grow buckwheat, maize and beans. Rice they grow only to manufacture it into liquor, of which they are inordinately fond. They wear the scantiest of clothing. The States of East and West Mainglong, which are administered by the Superintendent of the Northern Shan States, are principally inhabited by Was, who are considered to be tame in comparison with their more independent brethren. Nevertheless, they have given considerable trouble from time to time, and their Sawbwas have anything but an easy time. Other tribes who inhabit the Shan States are :

RIANGS, OR YINS, as the Burmans call them. They are supposed to be Karens.

HKA MUKS, HKA MEIS, AND HKA KWEMS.—These also are supposed to be Karens. They all speak different dialects. The men now dress like Shans. The women wear petticoats with horizontal strips of colour.

These tribes are usually found in forests.

TAUNGTHUS.—The Taungthus form about one half of the population of the Myelat. The State of Hsahtung (Thaton) is almost entirely inhabited by them. The Sawbwa is a Taungthu.

The women wear a peculiar dress, with their hair dressed very high on the head.

TAUNGYOS.—The Taungyos live in the south of the Myelat. They are allied by descent to the Taungthus, only the Taungyo women wear red camisoles, whereas the Taungthu popular colour is black.

DANUS.—The Danus live on the borderland between Burma and the Shan States, and are more or less Burmanized.

INTHAS.—The Inthas, who, as I have mentioned, originally came from Tavoy, live on the Yaung Hwe Lake and its borders.

HPONS.—The Hpons live between Bhamo and Sinbo, and in the Namkam Valley, south-east of Sinbo.

KADUS.—The Kadus are half-breeds between Burmans and Shans.

LAHUS.—The Lahus live in Kengtung and Kengcheng. Their peculiarity is that they use the crossbow as a weapon and shoot poisoned pellets.

Then, there is a tribe called the LISHAW, who live in the North Hsenwi, and another tribe of AKHAS, who live in the Kentung State.

PANTHAYS.—The Panthays come from China, and their

principal town is Pan Long, in the Sonmu State. They are Muhammedans, and their chief industry is carrying. They own large numbers of mules, and are very sturdy and independent. The Panthays rebelled against China, and were not subdued till after a war which lasted from A.D. 1855 to 1873. At one time they had a Sultan of their own, and the last Panthay Sultan's heir is an exile in Rangoon.

I have mentioned all these tribes, of some of whom but little is known, to give you an idea of the great diversity of tribes inhabiting the Shan States, and it is a curious sight to see the representatives of so many different tribes assembled together on a market day in any of the Shan towns. As the women of the different tribes all wear a distinctive costume, the sight is an interesting one.

KACHINS.—The next tribe I will mention are the Kachins, otherwise called Chingpaw or Singhpo. They are so numerous as to form a small nation.

The area of the Kachin Hills under our administration is 19,177 square miles. Further north, latitude 28°, the country is unexplored. The Kachin Hills range from 1,000 to 12,000 feet in height above sea-level. The Kachins live mostly in the hills to the north, east, and west of Bhamo and Myitkyina districts, and in the Ruby-mine district. They also occupy the Hukong Valley, which is fifty-four miles long and thirty-five miles broad. The main road between Burma and Assam lies through this valley, in which there are many rubber forests. The rubber is extracted by the Kachins for sale to Chinese merchants, and the method of extraction is so wasteful that the trees are fast being destroyed. The Hukong Valley is as yet unadministered.

The Kachin administered country is under an Assistant-Superintendent, whose headquarters are at Sinlumgaba, in the Kachin Hills above Bhamo, and who is under the orders of the Deputy-Commissioner of Bhamo. For administrative purposes the Kachin Hills are divided into forty tracts. The law in force is the Kachin Regulation. The Kachins were a very wild and savage people when we first came into contact with them, occupying the hills between Burma and China; they raided both countries impartially. They levied blackmail on all traders passing through their country, and thus greatly impeded trade. They were also continually at variance with each other, and there was no law or order in their country. The Kachins are of Tartar origin. They are short and sturdy.

The Kachin tribes are numerous, and the principal are:

Marip	Lahtaung	Lepai	Maru
Nhkum	Marans	Sassans	

There are two divisions of Kachins—Kamsa Kachins, who are ruled by chiefs called Duwas, and Kamlao Kachins, who are republicans and recognise no chiefs.

At the death of a chief he is succeeded by his youngest son. The elder sons generally move away and found villages of their own. Their houses are substantially built with teak posts, bamboo mat walls, and thatch roofs. The houses are very large, extending from 100 to 150 feet in length, and often contain three generations of the same family. The roof at the general entrance extends over an open enclosure, in which pigs are penned at night. The Kachins wear dark blue or blue and green check, and every man carries a small bag slung over the left shoulder. The bags are of dark blue, or red cloth embroidered with red, green, and yellow. The women wear a skirt formed of broad alternate bands of dark blue, red, and white stripes, with prettily embroidered borders. They wear their hair in knots, covered by a coloured cloth, and in their ears they wear cylinders of silver or amber, from 4 to 5 inches long. The men are armed with guns, crossbows, and spears 6 to 7 feet long. Each man carries a formidable *da*, or sword (*linkin*) squared off at the end and narrowing to the top. It is carried across the right shoulder and hangs on the left side. There is a flat sheath, on which the weapon is kept in its place by bands of cane. The Kachins are very superstitious, and their only religion is spirit-worship. Their priests are called Dumsas, and are supposed to be inspired by spirits.

Blood feuds are kept up for many years, and unless settled by payment or compensation, are never forgotten.

The pacification of the Kachin country was not achieved without much fighting, and required considerable perseverance.

In 1888 the Kachins attacked Mogaung, but were repulsed with loss. In 1888–1889 the Kachin country was visited by several columns, and military posts were established at important points to dominate the country. In 1889 General Sir George Wolseley commanded an expedition against the Ponkan Kachins. There were various encounters with the Kachins up to 1893, when the construction of a post at Sima met with much opposition, and it required a concentration of three columns of military police to subdue the Kachins and complete the building of the post. Since 1893 the Kachins have behaved well, and are now fairly quiet, but are often difficult to restrain from attacking the Kachin tribes subject to China. These Kachins raid the Kachins who are subject to Burma, and our Kachins can never understand why they are prevented from retaliating.

A conference with the Chinese authorities was held in 1890-1891, and an agreement arrived at by which the officers on both sides meet every year and a general settlement of disputes between the Kachins on opposite sides of the border is arrived at.

The Chinese Kachins are under little restraint, and are almost invariably the aggressors. Our officers were instructed to assist the Chinese in preserving the peace whenever help is asked for and can be usefully given.

THE CHINS.—The Chins occupy the mountainous region on the west of Burma. Their country lies to the west of the Chindwin River, and is about 250 miles long and from 150 to 100 miles broad. Its approximate area is 10,250 square miles. The Chins were estimated in 1898 to number about 89,620 souls, and the numbers of the different tribes are as follows:

Tashons	39,215
Hakas	14,250
Soktes	9,005
Tlangtlangs	4,925
Yokwas	2,675
Siyins	1,770
Independent Southern Tribes ...	17,780
	89,620

According to the census of 1901, the number of the Chins was taken at 95,497. The Chins are of Tibetan origin, and are allied to the Nagas and Kukis of Assam.

The different tribes of Chins have each a separate dialect. The Chin Hills range from 4,000 to 8,000 feet in height. The villages are usually built on terraces, and surrounded with bamboo or thorn hedges. The approaches to the village are spiked with sharp bamboos.

Water is brought to the villages by aqueducts made of bamboo. The houses are built of pine planks and roofed with thatch. They generally consist of three rooms. The principal room is a half-closed porch, adorned with skulls of animals killed in the chase, or of domestic animals which have been slaughtered in sacrifice

The Chins are well-built, muscular men, and average 5 feet 6 inches in height. They are very much given to drink. They distil beer and spirits from millet, which they place in an earthen vessel and drink through long straws. The Chins are not given to much washing, and wear the merest apology for clothing. When at work in the fields they divest themselves of even that apology.

Amongst the Southern Chins the women's faces used to be tattooed black. This was to prevent their being carried off in raids by marring their beauty. This beauty I did not observe myself amongst the Chin women, even when not disfigured by tattooing. The habit is now dying out, as liability to be carried off in raids is much reduced under the British Government, except amongst the independent tribes.

The Chins were the terror of the Burmans who inhabited the country at the foot of the hills, which was almost depopulated. I remember when I was at Kindat, on the east bank of the Chindwin, in 1886, the Chins attacked a village on the west bank at dawn. By the time the troops could cross the river the Chins had killed all the men and carried off the women and children, and the troops were unable to overtake them. Such raids as this were of constant occurrence. The Chins are spirit-worshippers, and all their ceremonies conclude with a feast, at which there is much drinking, and the drinking often terminates in a fight, which is frequently deadly, as all the Chins are armed.

When we took the country every man had a gun —usually a Tower-stamped flintlock. They also carry swords, spears, and bows and arrows. They have a nasty habit of taking nicotine, obtained from the bowls of pipes, into their mouths, and any tribal arrangement come to is concluded by taking of nicotine into the mouth. This custom has had very alarming effects on British officers, who have been offered nicotine to seal a treaty, and have taken it in ignorance of what it really was.

It took the British Government from 1887 to 1894 to pacify the Chin country, and this result was only achieved by withdrawing the guns from the Chins. The Chin Hills were not considered part of British India until they were so declared for the first time in 1895.

The Chin Hills are administered by a superintendent with five assistant-superintendents. The law in force is declared by the Chin Hill Regulation of 1896. The law in force is the same as the law in Burma, so far as persons other than Chins are concerned. As regards Chins, the criminal law is the same as the law in Burma, with necessary modifications. The civil and revenue law of Burma does not apply to the Chin Hills, as the Chins are at too low a stage of civilization to require it. A few simple provisions of the Chin Hills Regulation and the rules thereunder suffice for the Chins.

The Pakokko Chin Hills are not under the Superintendent of the Chin Hills, but are administered by an Assistant-Superintendent under the orders of the Commissioner of Minbu.

The Chin Hills are a most trying country to travel in. The hills are very steep, and are separated by deep valleys. You see a village on an opposite hill, which seems to be a few hundred yards off, and have to travel up and down steep hills sometimes eight or ten miles to get to it. In many instances it is impossible to ride, as the roads are so steep. The country is, however, often well wooded, and in the spring, when the rhododendrons are in flower, it is well worth a visit.

Of late years much has been done to improve the road, and road-making has been a great factor in the pacification of the country. The Chins, who were considered so terrible by the Burmese, are now ordinarily law-abiding and well-behaved. Schools have been started to educate them, and they are being encouraged to take to trade and cultivation. A few guns have been left them for the purpose of sport and keeping down wild beasts, but all such guns are registered and stamped. The Chins submitted very badly to being deprived of their guns, and even after they were first taken from them they replaced them by purchases from Assam and Manipur Chins. The freshly-acquired guns were again taken, and they have now realized that they will not be allowed to retain firearms.

The Chins' method of warfare against our troops was to fire from an ambush, and then disappear down a steep hill, where our troops found it difficult to follow them, and this mode of warfare was exceedingly harassing to the troops, as may be imagined. The revenue paid by the Chins consists of a small sum per house, and is very inconsiderable. There are no troops on the Chin Hills now, which are held by the Chin battalion of military police.

I have now told you as much as time will allow about the tribes on the frontiers of Burma. I am afraid you may have found the subject wearisome, but I trust I have given you an idea of how very varied the tribes of Burma are.

In course of time the peculiar customs and dress, and,

I suppose, many of the languages and dialects now in use, will disappear, and I think much useful work has been done by our officers in preserving records of the distinctive characteristics of the tribes. Much information has been collected by Sir George Scott, Mr. Carey, C.I.E., and others.

There is, of course, a great deal more that I could have told you about these tribes, but my time is limited, and I have made my remarks as short as possible. If anybody should wish to learn more about these tribes, the 'Gazetteer of Upper Burma,' by Sir George Scott, and the 'Gazetteer of the Chin Hills,' by Mr. Carey, might be studied, as they contain most of what is known as yet of the tribes who have been so briefly mentioned to-day.

Sir George Scott has recently published a handbook of Burma, in which he gives a great deal of information about the tribes, accompanied by photographs of many of the most interesting types. Any of my hearers who wish to pursue the subject further might study this book with advantage. It is published by Alexander Moring and Co., of 32, George Street, Hanover Square.

DISCUSSION.

The Chairman said: We have listened to a very admirable paper, put before us by one whose long experience of Burma, both as Chief Commissioner and more recently as Lieutenant-Governor, entitles him to our absolute trust in the facts which he has enumerated to us. I can only hope that the paper, especially when it is published in our 'Proceedings,' will correct wrong impressions of Burma which are current in this country. As Sir Frederic Fryer pointed out in commencing his paper, the usual idea in England is that Burma is a land of rice and rivers, and that the inhabitants are a people who are remarkable chiefly for their gaiety and their picturesque attire. It is quite true that a bountiful Providence does supply Burma, particularly Lower Burma, with food obtainable with a minimum amount of labour, thus enabling its men to lead a happy life, to wear very gay clothes, to smoke long cheroots, and to leave most of the work to their womenkind. No doubt this is esteemed an earthly paradise—I mean for the men. (Laughter.) But Sir Frederic Fryer, by telling us so much of the frontier tribes of Burma, has enabled us to form a truer and more complete picture of the province. He has given us some conception of the difficulties we have had since the annexation of Upper Burma in settling the wild tribes, and he has shown the great measure of success achieved in these efforts. Sir Frederic alluded to some aspects of the subject more than once, but I could have wished that there had been time for him to have entered into more detail as to the simple protective administration we maintain over those interesting tribes, the Shans, the Chins, and the Kachins, in whose country our officers, civil and military, work together at what we may call the outposts of Empire. You will agree with me that there is no finer example of the work performed for civilization than that which is afforded by the sight of our civilians and soldiers working together for the benefit of these wild tribes and the inhabitants of Burma generally, and for the maintenance of the *pax Britannica*. (Cheers.)

Major-General M. W. E. Gosset said: Having held a command in Burma some years ago, I may, perhaps, give you a few traits of native character which came under my experience.

The Karens and other border tribes are not bad material for soldiers, and are amenable to discipline, whereas the Burman proper is not so constituted. When I was at Mandalay there were some companies of Burman sappers and miners, among which there were many men who would absent themselves for days together, and be recorded accordingly as deserters; they would then, as a rule, turn up, and when brought before their commanding officer and asked the reason for their absence, would often say, 'I went to a *pwè*' (a theatrical performance), which they seemed to think was quite an adequate and reasonable explanation for unauthorized absence. They were surprised under the circumstances that they were not let off, and could not understand that discipline must be observed.

With regard to the fighting capacity of the Kachins, we had good opportunities of testing it when, during my first year in Mandalay, I had four columns out doing very difficult work in mountainous country thickly wooded, where there were no roads, only narrow, rocky paths, often on the edge of steep cliffs. It is not easy for armed men to make their way along these mountain paths, particularly when the natives have built stockades to obstruct the passage. If it was not that they never very bravely defended these stockades we should have had much more difficult work than we had. One of the most remarkable instances of their giving way was when Lieutenant MacMunn, R.A., had to march with a convoy to a fort at Sadōn. On arriving at a river some seventeen miles from his objective, he found that the Kachins had put up stockades on the opposite bank, from which they opened fire on his small escort, comprising only thirteen Goorkhas and a native Punjabi officer. They had with them some twenty mules, carrying ammunition and supplies. Lieutenant MacMunn gained a small island on the river, and opened fire on the Kachins, who promptly bolted up their mountain path. The convoy pursued them for the whole seventeen miles, taking one stockade after another. At the village of Sadōn, half a mile from the fort, the young officer was shot through the wrist, and the Punjabi officer through the chest; but he carried his mules and supplies along, with the loss of a few mules. I think it was one of the finest achievements of a small party I ever heard of. The incident shows that even in their own country, where they have great natural topographical advantages, the Kachins did not make a very determined stand.

Sir Frederic Fryer alluded to spirit-worship among the Shans. On one occasion on tour I stayed at a rest-house in the vicinity of works in progress for the construction of a road. The natives of the village had built a dam across the river for the irrigation of their fields, and at each end of the dam was a little bamboo erection for the abode of *Nats*, for the Burmans, though nominally Buddhists, are really worshippers of *Nats*, or spirits. The Hindustani coolies, road-making under the Public Works Department, used the dam as a short cut. The headman of the village came to me and said if people were allowed to walk across the dam the *Nats* would be angry, the dam would break, and they would lose their crops. I interviewed the superintendent of the work, and told him the dam must not be used as a pathway, much to the relief and gratification of the villagers, who were very pleased that the anger of the *Nats* had been averted.

Dr. Cotterell Tupp, I.C.S., said : I only wish to say a few words about the Singpho Shan and Kachin tribes on the extreme north-east frontier of Burma, opposite to China. There is between the British frontier at Bhamo and the Chinese frontier near Manwein a strip of rugged mountainous country, inhabited almost entirely by Kachins, and to the north by Singphos. These people are, or were till quite recently, tribes of the most savage and barbaric kind. All our explorers who have penetrated to Burma from the north-east, either from China or from French Indo-China, say that by far the most difficult part of their journey was the strip varying from 40 to 150 miles between the Chinese and British frontiers. Nearly all these explorers were reduced to the last stage of misery and destitution, and were constantly in imminent danger of being murdered as long as they were in the Kachin territory. Margary and Colquhoun from China and Prince Henri D'Orléans from Tong-king all travelled in comparative peace and comfort in China and in Indo-China till they came to the Kachin frontier. From that time all their accounts are full of the miseries they suffered, the starvation they endured, and the constant threats of violence and murder which they encountered. Margary, the first European (at any rate, in modern times) to cross from China to Burma by this, the old trade route, which had been used from time immemorial for trade between China and Burma, travelled in 1874 under the protection of Chinese passports from Pekin, and was not only safe, but was well-treated till he came to Manwein. Thence to

Bhamo he was plundered, ill-treated, and constantly threatened, and escaped with difficulty across the frontier to Bhamo. He returned a month later as an *avant-courier* to Colonel Horace Browne's exploring expedition to China, and was brutally murdered near Manwein. This murder was inquired into by Colonel Browne, and afterwards by the Grosvenor Mission, and all agree that it was committed by the Kachins, and not by the Chinese. In 1882 Mr. A. R. Colquhoun travelled safely with his friend Wahab all through Yunnan from Canton to Manwein, but when they got into the Kachin country between Manwein and the Irawadi they were plundered, delayed, badly treated, and expected to be murdered every minute till they crossed the British frontier. Prince Henri D'Orléans coming from Tonking in 1895 was very nearly starved to death and murdered in these same savage territories. Indeed, every traveller has the same story to tell of barbarity, truculence, dishonesty, and savagery. Prince Henri came out at Sadiya in Assam, much further north than Bhamo. The reason why I have drawn your attention to this savage strip of territory and its inhabitants is that it is the only obstacle to opening up the old trade route from Burma to China, viâ Bhamo and Manwein. I am glad to learn from Sir F. Fryer that military posts have now been established in these regions, and they should do much to remove the hindrance to the re-establishment of the trade route. No doubt, however, much remains to be done, and I can scarcely credit the statement made by the *Globe* newspaper in May last that a light railway had been sanctioned from Bhamo to Momein. The construction of such a line would not be possible until the savage tribes on the Yunnan frontier had been subdued. Apart from the question of the trade route, it is to be hoped we shall take all the Singphos, Kachins, and Shans definitely under our control, not only for the purpose of civilization and good government, but in order that we may join our territory to the Chinese frontier without any gap between, and that, in case the French extend north and north-west through the Siamese Shan States, we may have a strong and defensible frontier there, including all the tribes which used to be called the Independent Shan States. Now that the borders of Burma, Siam, and French Indo-China are rapidly coming to a meeting-point far west of the great River Mekong, it is our evident destiny to govern among us —divide them how we may—the savage and unruly tribes on these important frontiers. (Cheers.)

Colonel Bingham said: I lived amongst the Karens for many years, and I am inclined to think that their good qualities have been generally overlooked. They may not be good fighting material, such as is obtainable in India, but I consider that they have a place to fill in the defence of the north-east frontier. They are excellent scouts, and with discipline and training we could make very reliable bodies of Karen scouts. The Karens are the only wild race of people in that part of the world that I lived amongst for any length of time, and therefore know really well, though, of course, my work brought me into contact with most of the other tribes.

Sir Thomas Holdich: I have never had the pleasure of serving in Burma, and therefore cannot give any personal reminiscences. The lecturer has well illustrated to us the extraordinary complexity existing in the ethnographic conditions obtaining on the Burmese frontier, but I think you will find corresponding complexity along the whole frontier of India. He has shown us that the original stock from which these different tribes are derived apparently came from the East—*i.e.*, from China—or from the North, and I take it that so far as the tribes of the northern and eastern frontier of Burma are concerned that must be so. But (a little apart from the subject of this paper, perhaps) I should like to ask if there is no evidence in Burma, and particularly Lower Burma, of immigration by sea, of either Malay influence or Tamil influence. And there is one other point about which I should like to have the latest information. You will see by the map that the head of the Brahmaputra in the Assam Valley is parted by only a very small distance indeed from the Upper Irawadi. Some time ago an expedition was formed to explore the intervening country, to discover whether there was any possible crossing of it, with a view to the construction of a railway between Assam and Upper Burma. The country was precisely what Sir Frederic has described—chains of high mountains, with deep and narrow valleys in between, presenting altogether insuperable obstacles to the advance of an army, and almost barring anything in the shape of railway construction. But since then great progress has been made in the surveys of Upper Burma, and I should like to know whether, within the last ten years or so, any better way of communication between Upper Assam and Upper Burma has been discovered. That, to my mind, is one of the most interesting problems of the future in connection with Burma. (Hear, hear.)

In replying to the discussion, Sir Frederic Fryer said: I should first like to reply to the interesting remarks of Dr. Cotterell Tupp. The Kachins have now been brought into such a state of tranquillity that they have abandoned attacking travellers and traders. From Bhamo to Tengueh there has been made a mule-road, along which mules or pack-bullocks can pass. This road is patrolled, and traders can now pass along with perfect safety. We made the road a few years ago as far as the limits of British territory, and the Chinese applied to us to carry on the work across the border. When I left Burma we were awaiting the Chinese contribution to carry out the work. They said they were perfectly willing to provide all the labour required, and would allow our engineers to make the road for them. I think the road is probably completed now. Since I left it has been decided to make a light railway along the road. The line can easily be constructed—there are no very difficult gradients—and I should think that in the course of a few years we shall see a railway from Bhamo to Tengueh. I forgot to say in my paper that the Kachins, of whose unruliness we have heard this afternoon, make excellent soldiers under proper training. We raised two companies of them for the Bhamo battalion of the military police, and one of these companies was sent as escort to the British representatives on the Burmo-Chinese Boundary Demarcation Commission. During this demarcation three of our officers went without a proper guard into a Wa village on market-day, and the Was turned upon them, killing two, while the third only narrowly escaped death. With the Chinese troops and the military police there was a detachment of the Durham Light Infantry. There was a sharp battle with the offending Was, in which the Kachins very much distinguished themselves. Meanwhile the soldiers of the Durham Light Infantry and the Kachins had become bosom friends, and nothing delighted the Kachins more than to get some of the Durhams to drill them. The men are very good fighters, and they readily submit to discipline, and I think we shall find that the Kachins will contribute a very considerable contingent to the military police before long. (Hear, hear.) As to a railway between Assam and Upper Burma, a survey was made—or, rather, a reconnaissance—through the Hukong Valley, and it was found that a railway could be made through that fertile valley without any great difficulty. But, of course, it would involve a very wide circuit to come from India right up the North of Assam, and then down the Hukong Valley, and then down from Mogaung, where there would be connection with the existing railway giving access to Rangoon. Lately there was a survey for a line from Burma to India coming east of Nimbu, but that was found to be very difficult and expensive. The last idea when I left was to make a railway from somewhere about Prome, past Akyab, to join up with the Chittagong Railway. A survey was started to ascertain whether a line was possible. It was feasible, but, owing to the number of rivers which come down along the coast, the line would have been a very expensive one indeed. In answer to Sir Thomas Holdich, I may say that there has been very little migration into Burma from India or the Malay States. Large numbers of Madrasis do come to Burma, but they generally come only for a season's work of gathering in the rice or working in rice-mills, and when they have made a sufficient sum of money, they generally go back to India. The Malays do not seem to have any great tendency to come to Burma. On the other hand, a good many Burmans are settled in the Malay States. There has been a large migration from China into Burma, and there are many Chinese in Burma, Chinamen having come from the province of Yunnan and settled in Upper Burma. I had several applications from Chinamen for grants of land. We were rather reluctant to meet these wishes, owing to the character of the Kachins; but now the tribes have been got into something like order the Chinese might, I think, be encouraged to come. They are very good and industrious cultivators, and orderly as a rule.

The Chairman, in concluding the proceedings, said: Sometimes we have discussions which are somewhat controversial in character, but there has been nothing of the kind to-day. The remarks made have been in expansion of the facts brought out in the paper, and we are unanimous in our appreciation of the lecture. Burma must always be a land of the deepest interest to us. As you know, the annexation of Upper Burma was forced upon us by circumstances on which I need not dwell. A point to remember, however, is that in these regions British and French interests meet, and our territories touch. Those who wish to add to their information on the subject of French interests in that part of the world may be referred to Dr. Cotterell Tupp's lecture in this room only last May. In a very interesting paper he dwelt upon the French in Indo-China. The annexation of 1886 took place in the vice-royalty of that wise, brilliant, and splendid statesman Lord Dufferin. The forebodings heard at that time, and which were uttered by many who perhaps did not know much of the subject, have been proved to be ill-founded. In Upper Burma both revenue and population have increased under the Governments of Sir Charles Bernard, Sir Frederic Fryer, Sir Hugh Barnes, and the present Lieutenant-Governor, Sir Herbert White. At the Mandalay Durbar in 1901 Lord Curzon, speaking of the stages of development from conquest to order and peace in Upper Burma, and of the way the more recent stages had been supervised by Sir Frederic Fryer, said: 'I cannot conceive a prouder reflection with which an Indian administrator can leave these shores than that he has nursed so sturdy a child of Empire from childhood to adolescence.' I think our society is to be congratulated upon having had from the administrator of whom this was said a paper so full of detail on an aspect of Burmese affairs but little known. In preparing such a paper there is a vast amount of labour in the way both of collection of material and of compression. I propose, therefore, that we should accord Sir Frederic Fryer a cordial vote of thanks for his excellent and informing paper. (Cheers.)